IN A CHILD'S EYES

Written by Melanie Maddy • Illustrated by Celia Marie Baker

**To my grandparents who encouraged long walks,
storytelling and making a mess in the kitchen.**

-M.M.

**For my parents
who sent me outside to play.**

-C.M.B.

Text copyright © 2014 by Melanie Maddy
Illustrations copyright © 2014 Celia Marie Baker

All rights reserved. Published by Crazy Heart Publishing.
No part of this book may be reproduced or transmitted in any form or by any means, electronic or mechanical, including photocopying, recording, or by any information storage and retrieval system, without written permission from the publisher.

First Edition
10 9 8 7 6 5 4 3 2 1
Printed in USA

Summary: A day at the river with a grandfather and grandson finding treasures and enjoying each others company. A story about how life continues on with our children "Whether we falter whether we fly" life goes on in a Child's Eyes. Look and find hidden objects in specially marked illustrations. Book also includes sheet music and chord notation for the song. A music download of the song performed by Melanie Maddy can be purchased online at melaniemaddy.com/store

ISBN #978-0-692-20892-2

The art in this book was painted in watercolor.

Book designed by Celia Marie Baker

Text is set in Palatino

ebook and paperback versions available at www.melaniemaddy.com

LOOK AND FIND
Hidden images in the specially marked illustrations!

He was making his way up on over the rocks,
wearing those little, blue aqua socks.

Holding his Grandpa's
steady hand,
Spying a place
they'd sit in the sand.

Looking up the river with the trees on each side,

on to the mountains, on up to the sky.

He opened his small arms wide and said,
"I can see the whole world through my eyes!"

And they both knew, sure as a heartbeat,
between the two, a circle was complete.

And the life goes on;
on to the mountain,
up to the sky.

And life goes on;
whether we falter,
whenever we fly.
The life goes on,
in a child's eyes.

Grandpa turned to the boy sitting there in the sand, seeing his joy made him feel young again.

As he rolled his pantlegs up with a grin, the boy jumped up and said, "I'm goin' in!"

And they waded that river
a good, long while.
Found every treasure,
shared every smile.

Then the boy said, "Grandpa, I know what I'll do;
When I grow up, I'm gonna be like you."

And they both knew,
sure as a heartbeat,
between the two,
a circle was complete.

And the life goes on;
on to the mountain, up to the sky.
And life goes on;
whether we falter, whenever we fly.
The life goes on, in a child's eyes.

In a Child's Eyes

♩ = 124

Introduction: C Csus C Am Amsus Am F Fmaj7 G Gsus/A G/B

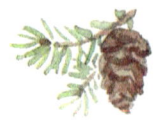

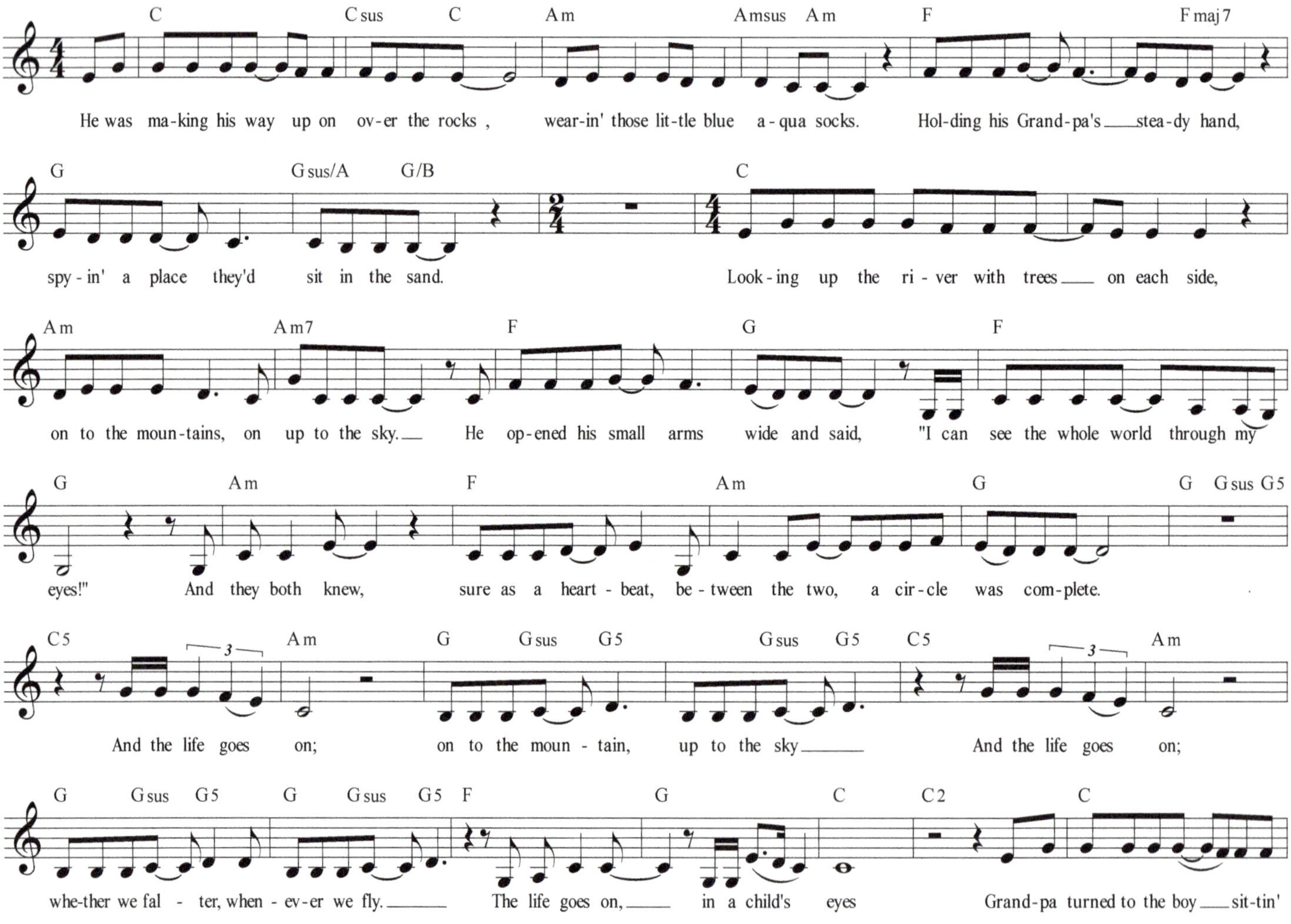

©

Sheet music by Jonathan Bletscher of Bletscher Transcriptions

Author

Melanie Maddy lives in a log home on Camano Island, Washington. She enjoys creating gardens, making salsa and entertaining family and friends around a bonfire.

She is a singer, songwriter, and author of her first children's book "In A Child's Eyes. The lyrics of a song she wrote about a little boy playing at the river with his grandfather which reminds us how, life goes on in a child's eyes.

For my children and grandchildren who keep me young at heart and fill my life with love, you are amazing!

Illustrator

Native to the great Northwest, Celia Marie Baker lives in Snohomish, Washington with her loving husband and their three energetic little boys.

Celia graduated from Cornish College of the Arts in 2008. She has illustrated several books for various local self publishing authors.

Thanks to a grandpa who let her take sips from his travel mug, Celia loves coffee. She also loves books and spending time with her family.

CPSIA information can be obtained at www.ICGtesting.com
Printed in the USA
LVOW02*0402180815
450298LV00011B/27/P